Is This My Final Form?

Also by Amy Gerstler

The True Bride

Primitive Man

Past Lives (with Alexis Smith)

Bitter Angel

Nerve Storm

Crown of Weeds

Medicine

Ghost Girl

Dearest Creature

Scattered at Sea

Index of Women

Is This My Final Form?

Amy Gerstler

PENGUIN POETS

PENGUIN BOOKS
An imprint of Penguin Random House LLC
1745 Broadway, New York, NY 10019
penguinrandomhouse.com

Set in TT Tricks Light
Designed by Sabrina Bowers

LIBRARY OF CONGRESS CATALOGING-IN-PUBLICATION DATA
Names: Gerstler, Amy, author.
Title: Is this my final form? / Amy Gerstler.
Description: First edition. | New York: Penguin Books, 2025.
| Series: Penguin Poets
Identifiers: LCCN 2024043970 (print) | LCCN 2024043971 (ebook)
| ISBN 9780143138488 (trade paperback) | ISBN 9780593512555 (ebook)
Subjects: LCGFT: Poetry.
Classification: LCC PS3557.E735 I8 2025 (print) | LCC PS3557.E735 (ebook)
| DDC 811/.54—dc23/eng/20240923
LC record available at https://lccn.loc.gov/2024043970
LC ebook record available at https://lccn.loc.gov/2024043971

Printed in the United States of America
1st Printing

The authorized representative in the EU for product safety and compliance
is Penguin Random House Ireland, Morrison Chambers, 32 Nassau Street,
Dublin D02 YH68, Ireland, https://eu-contact.penguin.ie.

For Alexis Smith (1949–2024)

ARTIST, MENTOR, FRIEND

Contents

When I was a bird,   3

I

The Bride of Frankenstein   7
Marigold   8
The Bible as Literature   10
Novice   11
My Witch   12
the meek   14
Mae West Sonnet   15

II

Étude   19
Finding Your Voice   20
The Story of Music   21
Some of Us Never Got Over It   22
Pucker and Fizz   23
Fourteen Sonnets   24

III

Schmaltz Alert   33
Mr. Moderation   36
The Fall   37
As Winter Sets In   38
Anticipating Spring   39
Behaving Truthfully Under Imaginary Circumstances   40
Siren Island   41

IV

For E.   55

Invention   56

Animal Light   58

Voicemail from Satan   59

One Who Is Always Arriving   60

The Lure of the Unfinished   61

Having checked the *Egyptian Book of the Dead* out of the library,   62

keep walking   63

V

The Cure   67

Downsizing   69

Postcard   70

Leniency Letter   71

Wound Care Instructions   72

Ode to the Pillow   74

Night Guidance   75

Night Herons   77

Acknowledgments   79

Notes   81

Internal division, mystical affinities, shape-shifting can be fertile; the way through the stone door needs many vehicles, plural morphologies, and metamorphoses . . .

—MARINA WARNER

Is This My Final Form?

When I was a bird,

my forward-drooping head plume bobbed
as I walked. I liked to conceal myself
among rocks. I broke bad news to bees
when needed. Dried feet of my species
were prized by museums, so our nests tended
to be tucked among cliffs. The best parts
about being a bird were absence of shame,
quick passionate mating, how my body
passed through yours mid-flight, and
the pinprick tickle of swallowing seeds.
Thus I lived, as bristle-thighed curlew,
red-moustached dove, bald ibis, or masked
shining parrot, my obvious gravitas noted
and admired. Why we died out I cannot say.
Later in the day I'll have a little think about
that, about how I keep mixing up worlds
now that the old answers no longer suffice.
A swift and reliable messenger, when I fell
I landed quite lightly, beneath the notice
of all but a handful of ants. One spring
I laid eggs with lavender spots. As a fuzzy
headed chick, my alarm call but an anguished
hiccup, I once observed a scurry of squirrels,
concealed in a hollow tree, wearing seventeenth
century clothes. Alas, no one believes me.

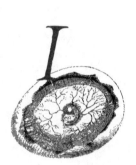

The Bride of Frankenstein

Late at night, I glimpse my ideal woman.
Problem is, she exists only on TV. Nonetheless,
I am smitten. Seams divide one perfect cheek
into three continents. Her impersonation
of an angry swan is so feral that I long
to fill my mouth with feathers. She walks stiffly,
this actress on stilts, as if her joints don't work.
Her eyes dart like a prey animal's. She's onscreen
only three minutes, yet in that brief time
manages to channel both startled newborn
and enraged, caged predator. A crumbling
puppet, her lipstick like ink, her legs were bandaged
so tightly on set, I read, that she was unable to move
and had to be carried. When the film opens, before
she becomes monster, she wears a white net dress
with sequins shaped like butterflies, moons, and stars.
Censors objected to the neckline of that gown.
What an ultimate striptease it would be if her
bandages peeled. She could continue to speak
swan, I wouldn't mind. On stormy nights our bed
would become an elevator, ascending the floors
of a blackened castle, bursting clear through
the roof, penetrating an electrified sky. In each
of her movies, I read, she was asked to scream.
Now, she screams without my even having to ask.

Marigold

I.

Today I'll listen to whatever music Spotify has in mind.
Concerto for Black Holes and Slime Molds by the Panty Sniffers?
That algorithm knows me so well! I've pitched myself under
this magnolia tree, heart-first, before I get lobbed anyplace
worse. No more of Grandpa's stuffed marlin glaring at me
from the living room wall. No more robocalls offering
to restructure debt never incurred. No more doomscrolling
(for the moment). I've retreated to the bosom of nature,
where bird chirps whir like sticks being fed into a wood-
chipper and magnolia leaves clatter into my lap like leather
wings. Mari has flown off to Mexico. She believes in UFOs.
She wants to be called Marigold now, to leave her sad past
behind and bask in the mysteries of sex and drugs
and panhandling and side hustles and *is that really so bad?*

II.

It seems really bad, or at least alarming to me, though
I, too, was a hot mess in my twenties, so long ago,
in a different era and circumstance. I'm still a sunken
ship riddled with eels. I'll admit that up front.
But since I'm using Marigold's trials and travails
as a thinly veiled excuse to blab about myself,
let's get back to her. Marigold's nose runs constantly.
She suffers from asthma and eczema. She loves animals,
toddlers, psychedelics, and girl bands. We share three
of these four loves, since I've been reduced by advancing
age to pretending I prefer booze to hallucinogens.
In the violent tides of her twenties, Marigold shed
the last of her baby fat, then graduated from stumbling
spiritual seeker to apprentice sensualist. *She wants, she wants . . .*

III.

She wants to spit in capitalism's tea, to impress older,
heavily tattooed fellow sensualists (the kinds who leave
teeth marks), kick patriarchy in the nutsack, darken
her hands with red and ocher dirts of other worlds,
learn five languages (but only by osmosis) while chasing
ninety-nine kinds of buzz and trying to pull free
from the tar pit of history. At her age, one is pure urge.
Life is a wildfire. So, it's no big sin that her bedroom
resembles a place where, among all their hoardings,
a pair of hoarders just staged a 24-hour wrestling match.
I just worry about her. Like I have the right, *me*,
who brims with wrongful convictions all day, then tucks
herself into bed each night with ten stuffed animals
and an Ambien sandwich. *So, what am I trying to say?*

IV.

Am I saying, Marigold, that in your attempts to enter
heaven you're crashing the wrong gates? That I wish
you'd find life-guiding messages someplace other
than in sidewalk scatters of pollen? Oops, I do
that, not you. Clearly projection is one of my sins.
Maybe your determination to get lost is a valid response
to any decade in which people feel they're about to be
vaporized daily. It's a crippling time to be young.
I want the magnolia to reach down its branches
and hug me. My twenties were a rapturous tantrum
during which I aspired to be lady, tiger, and pirate
rolled into one. When I try to recall that madness,
it seems like it never really happened, or as if it did,
to *someone*, but I'm not sure I was ever there myself.

The Bible as Literature

She clubbed her new husband to a pulp
with a fire extinguisher when she was young.
These things happen. Years later I met her
in a class called "The Bible as Literature."
We learned that books on scrolls unfurl
in just one direction, surging forward
like waves breaking. Paged books, however,
allow us to jump around in a narrative,
go back, leap ahead, as many of us ache
to do at times in our lives. Whether I
should have known that the way her face broke
into Cubist fragments as I tried to memorize it
was a sign she would soon turn the page on me,
whether despite her absence I continued
to love her in slow-dripping biblical
time, wracked by sky-cracking thunder
and slaked by puddled honey, or whether she
flashed in and out of my life like lightning, I will
not say. She needed to keep moving. If you can
make out the shape of her person from behind
this prison of horizontal bars (the lines of
this poem) you're a better man than I.

Novice

I have a strong wish to see god for myself,
so I surrendered my name. Anonymity suits
me. My soul is a perpetual request, a crumpled
candy wrapper. In chapel we lower our heads
and ask to be forgiven. I pray to be cured
of being me. Not quite ready to exit the sensual,
I gulp the mountain air as though it were claret.
I *really* like sweets. When I set my mug down,
I thank it for not disappearing. In the pocket
of the habit they gave me I find three pennies,
some petrified crumbs, and a black-and-white
snapshot of a boy and a small dog, though
personal photos are not permitted. Written
in pencil on the back: *Edward with Skippy*. I have
a strong wish to meet them both. My soul's
mother tongue is the language of no home.

My Witch

In winter, she wears a crown of whole cloves
strung on a loop of fishing line
she turns people into statues by laughing at them
her cat sleeps in a burnt cradle on silk pillows
her hair smells like a fireplace and she has no eyebrows
flowers bow down to her
she is an urgent, disheveled letter
her gaze has held for centuries
good books shed their petals in her hands
her lap is a moral impasse
she is god's and the devil's bitch
since in her body they collaborate
her heavy necklace of ambiguities does not weigh her down
she's a chainsaw ingenue
who rents an attic room twenty thousand leagues under the sea
she will bless your house and hasten the rain
most of the time she sleeps on the floor
birds perch on the tub's rim while she soaks her feet
she believes rum is a food group
she knows everything will disappear
she recites the old spells with new vigor
she doesn't judge the duplicity of the flesh
her clothes grow on trees
sparrows nest in her rafters
she says *being civilized is overrated*
she wears dark-blue suede kitten heels
and has long, disoriented hair
she floated past my ninth-story apartment window last night
punished, she says, is how she often feels
that morning back in third grade
when she was elected Little Miss Batcave
the weather grew peculiar

green clouds and a weird glow lit the sky
how frail, how puny we are she'll purr and then
did you feel that? did you feel the house shaking?
I may name a comet after her
strengthen me that I might do her bidding

the meek

They sit apart at parties, wilting
like neglected houseplants. Their music
is easily confused with white noise.
When the booze runs out, none
of them has the nerve to shoulder
into his coat and hike to a nearby
liquor store. You never catch
them wearing bright colors.
Their laughs are half-swallowed.
They yawn a lot, wallow in apology,
kneel, plead. Their sea of griefs
has been rising since humanity began.
So what's their plan? Most of the matter
in the universe is invisible, and the meek
teeter on the cusp of the unseen. When
we notice them at all, we're distracted by
bowed heads, tight smiles: benign disguises
behind which lurks an eternity of mildness,
and a ravening, saber-toothed surprise.

Mae West Sonnet

wicked, scandalous, bawdy, lewd, immoral, and oh so impure
is it not time for Congress to save the nation from Mae West?
unrepentant goddess wields liberation effects
chaos reigns if you reveal the hilarity of sex
she writes her own material
plays hooker as heroine
attends a séance or two
with frank sensuality
mom's a corset model
hordes of men tamed
virtue severed from gender
she soon got over being ashamed
Mae struts around in flattering gowns
intones in a smoky contralto: *show people you're scared and you're through!!*

II

Étude

As a child I loved air raid sirens and the blare
of the "all clear." The vacuum cleaner's roar.
The scrape of the dog's teeth raking a bone.
The rustle of mother's skirt as she was leaving.
All were melody to me. I wanted to test the outer
limits of listening. But what could that mean?
I took seriously the galaxies of static between
radio stations, full of whispered transmissions
from the living and the dead. I didn't have to
explain whether or not it was music. I just needed
to get there. So I tried, constrained by physical
limits, and the feeling, at times, of having failed
at life and let others down. People try to deny
their freedom. Freedom derived from emptiness
and silence is most scary to me, but also most
productive. In the no-man's-land between
noise and music, you can make sounds evolve
by doing things you were told you couldn't do.
Some of it was worked out mathematically. When
I read that giraffes hum to each other all night,
I thought, *That's just one example.* You can be the music's
protégé, make it echo in you. There wasn't a mad
scientist in sight, so I supposed I would have to do.

Finding Your Voice

Rain for a week. Atmospheric river, they say.
The dog nuzzles your hand. You haven't spoken today.
Go ahead, talk, no one is listening. The walls are not
listening. Nor are the mice living inside them.
Nor is the hyacinth in the kitchen, swilling
northern light. Tonight, your mind's shy
as an otter drying a saint's feet with her fur.
Is the dilemma not having a self, or possessing
too many? Some scrappy as cats in a bag,
others melting like drugstore chocolates,
plus selves who invade you by mistake, as though
they hopped on the wrong bus after midnight.
Can you let loose so powerful a sound now it stops
an egret mid-gulp, frog lodged halfway down
her throat? Could you call up a yowl to rouse
owls from their day-sleep, rattle leather-shelled
dinosaur eggs into hatching at last? Try. Sing out
a sentence that echoes on Pluto. Yodel a whole golden
record of musical quirks, just to see if your voice still works.

The Story of Music

Passionate discussions in cafés or dark bars
make their own kind of music also snowfall's
white silence or a mother humming to a baby
whose cries plunge its mother off obsidian
cliffs of another two a.m. feeding yes we need
songs to soothe kitchen ghosts who clank
forks and spoons believing that's opera
so please repeat your chorus of praise
for "ordinary happiness" till it's engraved
in my gray matter also chants warning
mourners to keep the dead dead plus rhymes
to ward off malaria and protect kids
from childhood diseases including suicidal
ideation as they play beneath canopies
of the remaining trees we spent centuries
crooning treble clef hymns to under our
breaths but that won't help the planet
or can it and who maps the paths music takes
as it snakes through our brains and can we
use those sacred channels to solve our problems
and do we need to become pagans again beg
the weeds' pardon pray to Nile crocodiles
and humpbacks who sing at the bottom
of the sea songs complete with whistles
shrieks and themes I hope they survive us
someone I love is smoking in the yard and
opened his mouth just now to catch hailstones
on his tongue melting bits of aberrant weather
dear Earth what's this persistent thrum
emanating from your core that harmonizes
discordant parts of my brain and can you
please explain what makes music music

Some of Us Never Got Over It

(ON WATCHING THE DIRECTOR'S CUT OF WOODSTOCK)

What were you fools trying to do back then? Hell if I know. Lay bare
our exceptional animal talents? Drown in the stickyfinger jizz
of the sixties? Chase revelation, as psychonauts always do?
Maybe we aimed to swallow the sun, become the sum of all
human knowledge. Infinite alternatives were blowin' in the wind.
Acid elongated our limbs. We mated and mated, grew extra-
sensory. No way we'd ever end up like our parents. We'd
wander the globe in flowing robes, maybe naked, seeking god's
raw thoughts, which we'd smoke or let melt under our tongues.
We'd unite with the Cosmic Mind, via art films, patchouli oil
(which I'd be pleased never to smell again), loud music, frantic sex,
and epidemic dance jags, during which many of us (including
those now dead) flipped pills into each other's mouths like the bean-
bag toss at a carnival. I guess we hoped to win some kind of prize:
world peace, true love, or a giant, huggable, fuzzy stuffed animal.

Pucker and Fizz

Poems are prophetic. Or mimetic.
Or eidetic or pathetic. Or regret-ic.
Or pleading. Poems can be free-
wheeling seas of molten feeling. Or
trance-inducing, corseted, or misleading.
Poems leave traces everywhere, as beasts
leave tracks upon earth and air with
wings and feet. Thank you, Poetry,
for protecting me from collapse, sack,
overthrow, and defeat. It was sweet
of you, Poetry, to invite me to dine with
the Society of Extinct Animals, hearty eaters all,
and each a fan, since their rise and fall,
of shouting into the annihilating wind.
Poetry, is it wrong for me now to break
my lifelong vow never to talk about Poetry
in a poem? But Poetry, from whence
do these fits of love assail me, as I watch
dogs slurp water, or when I sip a puckery
citrus fizz? Insistent as riptides, where
do these spasms of love for all that is
come from? My guts? My shrunk-
to-a-raisin brain? These sudden loves drive
me bonkers and save my bacon. But what
am I to do when seized by wracking
transports of adoration daily, in ways I
can't contain? Here, Poetry, you take them.

Fourteen Sonnets

1.

under Dad's prudish roof
texts ping into the inbox:
you've been acting odd lately
somebody's gonna get spanked!
please note personal quirks
in the space below:
list status as *loiterer* or *landlubber*
Father kept silent
so I sought garrulous lovers
inside night's scarlet quietude
and lacquered afternoons
please ignore threatening phone calls
from long-dead explorers
they suffered much

2.

black-clad pilgrims harsh our vibe:
pray your way out of it, wimps!
when personality goes numb
flattery becomes a kind of battery
wanna hear some crazy drama
about the invalid sister?
whining as though wounded
she lies on her side, a stove boat
crews of dry-hump abusers
play charades in her rigging
bare-knuckle brawls break out on her brow
don't let a pill-fueled Instagram rant
hurt your delicate feelings
yes, I'll have mezcal if you've got any

3.

o heart of my different ages
where's the monsoon you promised?
my sins were feather-light
before my boner exploded
take care, you who get caught red-handed
stealing long-held beliefs
don't let your hearts get lost in the sauce
as forests go velvet with moss
as the narrative picks up speed
as a tiny fetal horse practices galloping in the womb
I felt your kiss long before lips got involved
a distant gilded pucker
played on tin instruments
would it ruffle your feathers if I touched your aura?

4.

his giggle floated above all others
at the laughing academy
like cream on milk, nay, like xylophone notes
or voicemail from Satan:
"May I come over to frolic and gloat?"
a presumably gorgeous
fastidious vandal
yet not quite what I had in mind:
cold mutton suppers
threats left hanging for weeks
no wails, groans, or shrieks
just novels skimmed during lunch hour
burnt muffin crumbs
and ossified silence beholden to no one

S.

the naked body's opulence a million times true
booze flings open doors
she could flee through, maybe
the pomegranate tree hid her fruit
under long verdant skirts
you must not leave me until
I choose the very best merry-go-round horse
I have something to unbosom
before I repent of it
it begins with spitting
and ends with the whites of the sky
as seen from your bed
eruptive love
must be acted on before it burns away

6.

a coffee shop marquee taunts: *Spaghetti is Immortal!*
the waiter sets down your plate
wracked with homesickness
for an America that never existed
a lot of throbbing reported this winter
maple leaves eerily lit
birds asleep in short bursts
curses ringing in their ears
I was but a child in those years
voluptuous, haggard, beautiful
taking therapeutic baths
moving beyond known fuckeries
disruptions and alibis
dreaming of joining a great flock of comrades

7.

he sketched a map of the kingdom
with no ungentle hand
preached to the wheat
in grainy-voiced waves
ravished captives
and let eagles feed them
per the suggestion of an ascending friend
whose body thrums like a harp
hurled down a well
the funeral was hell
so tell it to me slowly
how a community of hermits
blinks on and off all night like fireflies
hence these tears

8.

if fingers don't work
find other ways to investigate her breasts
slobber on her dress
force the river to say *yes*
sip her residual fertility at your desk
or in a bootlegger's basement
its windows bereft
of salvage glass
shattered by lightning
as one minor god after another demands
we destroy what we'd loved:
marble, field mice, and mud
sick-ass clouds of insect witnesses
and any shred of eternity we had left

9.

one of his earliest masterworks
a vast black chasm
vanishes before your eyes
unmoved by your tears
or strict laws pertaining to magic tricks
in your ridiculous country
I have trouble memorizing everyone's girlfriend
being impelled to embrace them all
or saw them in half
makes me sleepy
till tequila sets me straight
bow to that lust before it's too late
it takes a while to wriggle out of that dress
please know: he is by no means done with us

10.

bonfires blaze on the library lawn
ours and ours alone
soft gold with apricot overtones
flaming beech trees dot the region
a woman's coat floats on the lake
is that a halo or a ring-shaped coffee cake?
please eat it for my sake
after he smashed his plate on the floor
I couldn't remember the Spanish Inquisition anymore
craving dirt under my nails
owls too numerous to count
and a shot of fossil pollen, I took my leave
no longer able to restrain my praise
for the fulsome bouquets of coming days

11.

from its first gurgle
that family was doomed
unhand me, sir, or I'll whack off an ear
she put all her love into exquisite dinners
as though she had no name on earth
despite the low manner of her birth
no one tortured her or made her path difficult
infinite and unaccountable friendliness loomed
bloomed its little heart out
then sank lifeless to the ground
meadows well up at the bottom of my cup
safe in my bliss
in an exclusive rooftop lounge peering down on all this
they say she never regained consciousness

12.

the bearer of this letter
(typhoons kaboom in his headphones)
is a tremendous new talent
who kissed me hard
wearing his "I've had five glasses of wine" face
he doesn't wish to be domesticated
so make him see stars!
but is it a present if he buys it for you with your own dough?
we return to our burrow in a rural graveyard
something ancient is happening
rinsed, bitterish, stricken
we shed our clothes
as woodpeckers chisel a nest
and dance uninhibited

13.

little girls cherish her protection
a swindler's widow
wildcat in human shape
headed in a less hysterical direction
negative confession, she said,
means deny everything
to escape their face-melting gaze
but don't scare them away
they're crocheting a sword and a shield for me
aboard the party barge
marooned by summer floods
turbulence and shock waves
forbidden to disobey or shake your fist
you can tell whoever the fuck you want to about this

14.

an entity old as the universe
kicked in the headlights of her car:
look how she blushes!
shrines sprang up like mushrooms
seconds after the explosion
canoes became the sole means of transport
jars of ancient light lit the way
through the rainforest like orchids
held aloft by a man with an extraordinary forehead
who shamefacedly weeps his way downriver
having murdered apple orchards back home
an anxious nation heads for the exits
though of course she could never express it
while the green sea flaps ceaselessly at your feet

III

Schmaltz Alert

One whole loaf of bread, a baguette
sliced lengthwise in half, though of course
they never say *baguette* in Vienna, they had
other words in that slightly grimy dark bar
where I first saw it displayed in a poorly lit
glass case next to a plate of what I mistook
for burnt chocolate cookies but which turned
out to be thin, crisp slices of blood sausage.
A jar of rubbery pickled eggs, blurred
in murky liquid, sat on top of the case.
But I was mesmerized by the sandwich.
What in god's name is smeared on that bread—
I almost said—*that translucent goo the color
of pus?!* For politeness' sake I asked in my
creaky German, *What's that sandwich in
the window?* Which probably came out
something like, "What is window-bread?"
But aided by my pointing, the guy behind
the bar received the meaning. He looked
as if I'd asked what beer was. *That's a chicken
fat sandwich*, he replied, as though to a dim
child. Yes, those were chopped raw
onions sprinkled on top of the schmaltz,
which was spread thick like peanut butter.
Like so many things my mother cooked
that I gave her grief for and wouldn't eat:
liver, tongue, parts of the animal I couldn't
bear to recognize, let alone ingest—
suffice it to say I was utterly repulsed
by the python-like sandwich sold in sections
at that tavern in the land of my ancestors,
and with my friends at the table, I laughed

at it. Yet, eating to keep warm—what did I
know of that in my privileged existence? What
did I know of pogroms, Russian winters, forced
immigration, of the value of fat, its anti-
starvation richness, of using every bit of a bird,
my picky-eater-hippie-vegetarian-college-educated
self refusing to acknowledge any such necessities,
wrinkling my nose at the stink of cabbage cooking,
squinting at Russian writing on the backs
of forebearers' multi-stamped passports slipped
into a photo album, their set, defenseless, nameless
faces peering at me hungrily. Once an uncle
at the wedding of his son, a skinny, hairy kid
who was marrying a Rubenesque beauty, said,
"He always did go for those little fatties," as though
this was a delightful remark. Actually, he
used the term "little fatties" as a second try.
First, he said *zaftig*, but based on what he read
as incomprehension on my face, he figured
he needed to translate for the poor dumb
Jewish girl who didn't know her own language.
But though I know little Yiddish, I was familiar
with *zaftig*, lobbed as a compliment among my
relatives to mean *a well-padded, curvaceous cutie—
nobody's stomach rumbling here!* An aunt took me
aside one afternoon when I was twenty, advising,
You should eat more, dear, if you want to catch a husband.
I didn't bother to respond or keep the contempt
off my *punim.* Anyway, old friend, what I
wanted to say is that on the phone the other day,
when you said *Schmaltz alert!* to warn me
you were about to say something affectionate,
I remembered that gross, noble sandwich
for the first time in years. I thought about how

we both come from Russian Jews who fled first
to Europe, where they perfected that sandwich
as well as an ability to simultaneously mock
and embrace the excessively sentimental, and
for no good reason I found myself in tears.

Mr. Moderation

After eating fourteen sausages for breakfast, Mr. Moderation had the meat sweats again. Then he got blotto on vodka instead of watching the baby, who climbed out of her high chair and began flinging mashed banana at the geriatric cat. When's the last time you had a shave, Mr. Moderation? Mushrooms erupt from the floor of your unwashed blue Ford. Cut to Christmas Eve. Mr. Moderation's been gobbling pot chocolates since ten a.m. Shellacked by noon, he partied hard on the laps of a tarnished goddess or three until, deep in the wee hours, it got shrieky. Neighbors called the cops. "I have no idea what happened here tonight, Officer," Mr. M. mumbles by way of apology. Sergeant Blackwood claps a hairy hand on the offender's back. "Take a drug holiday, for god's sake, man! Christmas or no, one more complaint and we'll have to run you in." Mr. Moderation used to be a gentle, breeze-tickled, flowery meadow of a fellow. But too much restraint erodes even the brightest minds. Over several decades, our once-moderate hero came to feel like a heap of Flamin' Hot Cheetos spilled onto the freeway, run over repeatedly by speeding 18-wheelers. Now he just wants to evict the dead embryos from his head so he can sleep. And he'd like to be reborn as someone he can actually stand. Why should his body feel like a sack of crumbling elephant tusks? And how did he transform from well-behaved underling to berserker at the peak of rutting season? Can't he just quit everything—his job, booze, fatherhood, etc.—and realize his boyhood dream to become an explorer wandering the globe, making discoveries that benefit all mankind, while still wearing his rocket pajamas?

The Fall

Determined to embrace whatever the world serves up, I stepped from the
car onto my driveway. In my head I'd been composing a fleet of emails
to my nearest and dearest: confessions, amends, heartfelt declarations.
I even addressed a few to myself: *Dear Princess Peashoot, Dainty Apricot
Macaroon, Lacy Maidenform Bra.* To impress my friends, I would season
their emails with phrases from Latin, such as *Magnificat anima mea
Dominum*, which means *my soul magnifies the lord.* The notion that souls
could zero in on what's holy and enlarge it, as telescopes do distant
planets, fortified me. Wondering how I might amplify the divine, I caught
my toe on a loose flagstone and took a pratfall. Bags I'd been carrying from
the art store went airborne. Paint containers crashed and exploded, so
that flagstones, grass, and especially the tan garage door became colorful
examples of random abstract expressionism. *Smash, splat, kaboom!* My
life's a cartoon. When I'm deep into making a painting, or just thinking too
hard, I forget I have a body, and lose track of the physical world. A fall is a
way for the landscape, pissed off at being ignored, to slap my face and say,
WAKE UP, MORON! As I lie on the driveway, noises swell. Everything above
me seems to sway. A butterfly flits by my head. Pushed this way and that
by invisible winds, butterflies pollinate 80 percent of land plants on this
planet. It strikes me that my prostrate position is an ideal place from which
to pray. Like any human cartoon character, I'd like to be able to fly. Not
every minute, just when the story calls for it. At least I'd like to be able to
stand, go inside, iodine my wounds, and submit to the comforting tongue
of my dog. I can hear the phone ringing inside the house. Guess I'd better
haul myself to my feet and see who's calling.

As Winter Sets In

One morning while brushing your teeth,
a strange face in the mirror. *Am I still in there?*
you ask. No reply. This face: a field in need
of reseeding. A corsage your blind date
sat on. A tattered map fished from the glove
box of a vintage car. At this age, every day
a new face you can't renounce or forsake.
Your job (you were told this as a child when
Grandma came to stay, as she could be mean):
summon the grace to make this face welcome.

Anticipating Spring

Mosses, pollens, and grasses tune up.
Can you listen without needing to speak?
That fox wants to tell you something. Drunk
on crumbs of the dead, roots sing. Blossoms
ache to flash their panties à la cancan girls.
Scholars mumble. Pages crumble. Wild
parrots scream between rainstorms. Slow-
growing saplings groan. Don't pray aloud.
Just wish from inside your hideout
of silence: *Ah, Goddess, please touch me.*

Behaving Truthfully Under Imaginary Circumstances

A yellow felt moon rises behind the scrim of night.
You stumble onstage to portray a sad, fanged beast
whose hide steams when he harms. People say
it's a great part. You're not so sure. Characters
make remarks you don't understand. You gnash
your teeth as fake volcanoes erupt and papier-mâché
leviathans spout fire. Other monsters tremble
in the wings. Bolts of blue cloth, held by black-clad
stagehands, are flapped to indicate raging seas.
The hero leaps off a mountain peak, tumbles
onto a feather bed tucked behind painted flats
of the Alps. You don't recognize this play,
your fellow actors, or the fur mittens you wear
to suggest paws. The statues in your palace:
intruders you turned to stone long ago.
A backdrop lifts to reveal trees and a road
dotted with crows, actually kids in crow suits
hopping foot to foot, singing and squawking,
picking at roadkill meant to represent their
inheritance, really a pile of rags and dried
toothpaste dyed red. One would like to have
little gifts on hand for the kids, candy or small
toys, but your costume lacks pockets. You don't
know your lines. Your roar squeezes a laugh from
tough customers in the balcony. At tomorrow's
matinee, maybe you'll take the stage naked,
remain silent till the clouds (cotton, cardboard,
and glue) begin drizzling genuine rain . . .

Siren Island

(a ten-minute play)

CHARACTERS:
SIREN JACK (man between 60 and 80)
SIREN DUFF (man between 60 and 70)
SIREN ED/EDNA (science nerd, gender-fluid, between about 30 and 50)
SIREN JULES (teenage girlfriend of Rommy)
SIREN ROMMY (teenage boyfriend of Jules)
SIREN MITRA (woman in her 60s)
JUNIOR SIREN (girl around 12 years old)

(An island with a palm tree more or less center stage. The rest of the stage is ocean. The Sirens sit or lie on the island. Their actions on land may indicate that the lower halves of their bodies are fishlike, perhaps akin to mermaids. In water they're more graceful. Jack and Duff are trying to crack coconuts with rocks. Ed is eating. Mitra is shading her eyes, scanning the ocean. She seems to be looking for something, which she does periodically throughout the play. All Sirens are present save Junior.)

JACK: Now don't you think that's overkill?
Gas and pills? That's showing off.

DUFF: The gas was just for backup, Jack.

(Duff's coconut finally splits. He does a sitting victory dance. Hands half a coconut to Jack.)

ED (*chewing*): I gulped a ton of meds and then
I tried to climb up to the roof.
Was good until the thirteenth floor.
Then I must have just collapsed.

JACK: Pick one means, folks. Then trust your choice.
And never second-guess yourself. (*Drinks coconut water.*)

MITRA: That's moot advice for this crowd now.

ED: OK, then Jack. So, what'd you do?

JACK: I am not like the rest of you.
Blind drunk, I drove into an oak.
An accident. I wrecked my brother's
precious Saab. He grieved that car
more than my death. *(A note in a bottle washes up. Jules retrieves it.)*

ED: The oak survive your rude assault?

JACK: The tree was fine.

DUFF: So, what's it say?

JULES: I'd rather not read this aloud.
Too weird and sad. *(Hands note to Duff.)*

DUFF: Ho ho. Get this.
(Reads.) JACK'S DEATH WAS NOT AN ACCIDENT.
JACK, FACE SOME FACTS. YOU LEFT YOUR EX
A SUICIDE NOTE.

JACK: I don't remember that at all.
But I was blitzed out of my gourd.
I do so mourn the loss of being
sloshed. Drunkenness perfected
me. It made me whole. I'm such
a fool about my feelings.

DUFF: I can relate. After a while
it got so I'd only attempt
to dance or fuck when I was high.
(Looks at Jules and Rommy.) It seems these two need no such help.
Can't you guys give it a rest?

MITRA: Now, Duff! That's mean. And watch your mouth.
There's children here.

DUFF: Children, my ass. They're sex cadets.
All they do is grope each other.

JACK (*moving close to Jules*): Cute chick like you, you want that guy,
who's barely old enough to shave
and mostly trout below the waist?
I swear, you make me salivate.
Please kiss me, Jules.
Just once. Just once. (*She recoils.*)

ROMMY: I'll fight you, sir!

MITRA: Let's calm ourselves. This island's small.

JULES (*takes Rommy's hand, addresses the group*): Know you all this: my love is true!
I find my passion's stirred anew
by these odd bodies we now wear.
Rommy is like the sun to me.
We only shared a bed but once.
Then we were quickly, cruelly parted.
A second chance, that's all we ask,
for he and I to be alone.

DUFF: So, we should leave? And where do you
propose we go?

ROMMY: We'd like you all to take a swim.
We need a break from prying eyes.

DUFF: A swim. That's rich.
Truth be told, I'd much prefer
to kick back here and just voyeur.

ROMMY: I'll fight you too, you loathsome goat!

MITRA: Oh, Duff, shut up and have a heart.
Ed, what's that fluff you're scarfing down
day in, day out? Reminds me of
the sugar floss my son once loved.
It was pale pink. They sold it at
the baseball game and county fairs.
What's that stuff called?

DUFF: Cotton candy?

MITRA: That's it!
(To Ed.) Be careful, it may make you sick.

ED: I've stumbled on a great new find
better than sweets, my gentle friend.
These Porifera, marine and green,
contain a psychedelic drug
to ease my agony of mind.

DUFF: Speak English, Ed.

MITRA: Porifera's the Latin name.
Ed's eating sea sponge, getting baked.
Does it make you hallucinate?

ED: For days and days. Sea sponges bruise
when roughly touched. Yeah. Just like us.
So don't start fights. You guys want some?
I'll get you stoned. I got a lot.

DUFF: It's tempting, but they look so gross.

JACK: How do they taste?

ED *(very high):* Uh . . . like a dolphin's silk pajamas?

JACK: That makes no sense.
We'll talk when you have sobered up.

ED: Not sure I ever want to be
sober again. I'll get you zonked.
Hangover free!

JACK: Maybe later.

JULES: What say you to our proposition?

DUFF: That we all leap into the drink
and swim around between the sharks

so you two kids can court and spark
till you are spent and fall asleep?
Nothing doing.

ED: I dive for sponges every day.
I've never seen a shark. Not once.

MITRA: Why can't we all give them some space?
Hasn't their suffering earned them that?

DUFF: All of us stuck on this bleached rock
have suffered much.
(Bottle with message washes up.)

ED (retrieves it and reads): SO TAKE A VOTE!

DUFF: The management has crap ideas.
OK. OK. All those who want
to let these randy infants rule
and push us off the only home
that we have known since we took leave
of prior lives, and make us plunge
into the ocean's roil and churn—

MITRA: You have a bent for melodrama.

ED: So roil and churn, so crash and burn,
so take your turn, so live and learn,
become a fern . . .

JACK: He's higher than the moon right now.

DUFF: I'm jealous, Ed.

ED: The moon, high noon . . .

JULES: Just two short hours is all we want.
Of course, you all will soon swim back.

JACK: If we survive.

ROMMY: Are you afraid?

DUFF: Damn straight, you selfish, lustful slug.

ROMMY: You froward and unable worm,
though swordless, yet I'll wring your neck. *(Lunges at Duff. Ed restrains
    Rommy. Jack is laughing at Rommy.)*

ED *(trying not to laugh too)*: Be careful now.
Can't see what there would be to fear
for any of us. We're dead already.

DUFF: You don't know what could happen next
if we get eaten or we drown.
We might end up someplace much worse
than this sunbaked, forsaken isle.

JACK *(still laughing at Rommy)*: Oh, Jules, what do you see
in this hotheaded turkey cock?
You need an actual man, like me,
to give you what you need.

ROMMY *(still being restrained by Ed, to Jack)*: Fatso, you're next!

MITRA: The three of you! Your macho antics
make me tired. Come on. Let's vote.
So, raise your hand if you are game
to let these lovers have some peace.
You promise that an hour or two
is all you'll need? *(Rommy and Jules nod.)*

JACK: That's so not true.
We'll never hear the end of this.
Pretty soon five times a day
and twice a night they'll bitch and moan
for all of us to "take a swim."
Everyone here knows how habit-forming
sex can be.

MITRA: Enough. Let's vote.

Who's ready to give them a break? (*Mitra, Ed, Jules, and Rommy raise hands. Jules and Rommy high-five each other.*)

DUFF: Jules and her dude don't get to vote!

No way is that OK with me!

ROMMY: I'll choke you now, with my bare hands.

MITRA: Chill out, young man.

OK. So fine. We'll vote again.

Rommy and Jules, you'll please abstain.

Who wants to give them what they ask? (*Mitra and Ed raise their hands.*)

DUFF: Who here votes NO? (*Duff and Jack raise their hands.*)

ROMMY (*to Duff and Jack*)**:** You scurvy, pigeon-livered toads.

I'll see you dead.

DUFF (*ready to fight him*)**:** The hell you will, you horny teen!

MITRA: Stop that or else.

The vote now stands at two to two.

And I'm not sure what we can do

to break the tie.

> (Junior Siren is seen in the water near the island. She looks drowned. She holds a stoppered bottle with a note in it. Mitra, Ed, Jack, and Duff wade in and pull her onto the shore. Mitra tries to revive her. Junior sputters, coughs up water.)

JACK: Where are we now, some nursery school?

How old are you? (*Mitra smooths Junior's hair, unwinds seaweed from around Junior's neck.*)

JUNIOR: Why thank you, ma'am. I'm twelve, I think.

DUFF (*takes bottle from Junior, reads message*)**:**

YOUR TIEBREAKER HAS NOW ARRIVED.

This pip-squeak? Someone upstairs

blew it again. She's too young to
have killed herself. And not near old
enough to vote.

JUNIOR: You're not the boss of this, you know.
This group of girls at school mocked me.
Every day. My hair, my clothes,
the way I talk. Prank-called my house
so late at night it drove my shaky
mother nuts. They photoshopped
my face onto creatures in stills
from monster films and posted those
results online. So, I—

MITRA: All right, my dear. Everyone here
knows what it's like
to want to end that kind of pain.

JUNIOR: You do?

ED: We do.

JUNIOR: Yeah? *(To Mitra.)* Even you?

ED *(moves next to Mitra)*: Tell her.

MITRA: I won't.

JUNIOR: I think that I might need to hear.

MITRA *(after a pause)*: I slit his throat and then my own.

DUFF: Say what?

JACK: Whose throat?

MITRA: My son's. Then mine.

JUNIOR: How old was he?

MITRA: He'd just turned three.

JACK: Oh no.

DUFF: But why on earth—?

ED: None of your fucking business, Duff!

JACK: That's heavy, man.

DUFF: You offed your child?

JACK: Mitra, that's wild.
I never would have guessed that *you*—

ED: Leave her alone!

JACK (*to Ed*): Don't get so sore.
(*To Mitra.*) Where is he now,
your little boy?

MITRA: I would give my soul to know.

DUFF: We haven't got souls anymore.

JULES: Oh yes we do.

MITRA (*indicating Junior*): When I first spotted this small child
bobbing out there, my heart seized up—

JULES: You thought 'twas him? Out in the waves?
Floating our way?

ROMMY: Your son? Dear lord. (*Takes Jules's hand.*)

MITRA: Day after day I watch for him,
pray he'll wash up onto our shore.
I think of very little else.

JUNIOR (*to Mitra*): I understand the thing you did.

JULES: Yes. We all do.

JACK: Not me.

DUFF: Or me. You can't forgive that kind of crime.

ED (*to Jack and Duff*):
Like you two mean old crusty fucks
have any sense what mercy is.
Why contemplate your own dark sins
when you can just gang up on her?

DUFF: No fair!

ED (*to Jack and Duff*): Want to discuss
who does and doesn't get absolved
for what they did? OK.
Let's talk about the tidal waves
of sickening grief you dudes unleashed
on those you knew when they got word
you'd snuffed yourselves.

JACK: What about you?

ED: I timed it so my wife would be
the one to find my corpse that night.
That it would be someone I loved
comforted me.
The damage my acts did to her—
the suicide and much besides—
well, let's just say I'm not immune
to having left a mess behind.

DUFF: Cheer up. No doubt by now
your wife's bounced back,
excited by some other guy.

ED (*to Jack and Duff*): Oh, thanks.
Even when you're not trying to be,
you two are cruel.
Good thing this drug can blunt my rage,
assuage my pain, erase self-hate,

and make of me a peaceful beast.
(Takes a chomp of sponge.)

JACK: Duff didn't mean—

ED *(offers Jack sponge)*:
Shut up and try a little bite.
It helps.
(Jack takes a cautious lick, then bigger bites.)
Everyone buzzed who wants to be?

JACK: Not bad.

DUFF: Now I'm depressed.
This conversation really stinks.
It makes me think of things I cannot
face, and dare not name,
cannot contain.
I need to rearrange my brain. *(Ed gives him a sponge. He eats.)*

ED: So now let's vote.
Who craves a bracing little swim
to gift our friends with privacy? *(Eventually, all raise hands.)*

JULES: Thank god! Thank you!

ED *(entering the water)*: I'll show you guys a coral reef.
It's got some rad cephalopods.

MITRA *(entering the water)*: Feels good. So warm. *(They both swim off.)*

DUFF *(to Jack)*: I can't believe we're doing this. *(Enters water.)*

JACK *(entering the water)*: The waves are like a strobe light show.
Rainbows exploding everywhere.
I guess I'm ripped. *(He and Duff swim off. Junior wades in and looks back at the island.)*

JULES *(to Junior)*: Go on. It's safe.

JUNIOR (*in the shallows*): But may I stay?

ROMMY: What for?

JUNIOR: To watch a bit and maybe learn?

ROMMY: Oh, great.
I'm sick to death of arguing.
What say you, Jules?

JULES: I say the little maid can stay,
if she remains farther offshore. (*Junior swims out farther, floats or treads water.*)

JUNIOR: Here good?

JULES: OK. (*Jules and Rommy embrace. They try to position themselves to have fish sex, are not sure what to do. Junior watches.*)

ROMMY: How can we—?

JULES: OW!
Not there, methinks. Wrong orifice.

ROMMY: How like you this?

JULES: Much better, love.
But maybe I should get behind?

ROMMY: Think that would work? (*They change position.*)

JUNIOR (*calls out to them*): You want to try it underwater?

(Rommy and Jules give no sign they hear Junior. The couple make various noises and expostulations like *How does that feel?* and *Good, my love!* as they try to get it right. Junior continues to watch as lights fade.)

IV

For E.

Pardon me for pretending I might wish
you back into existence so we could chat.
Better yet, I'd remain silent and bask
in the sound of your voice—music I'm
ashamed I can no longer quite call
to mind. I do remember your habit
of chattering your teeth in a cartoonish
manner when you got nervous or
bored. And I'm easily re-seized by how
keenly I once yearned to be your home
away from home, your quiet, tree-lined
street between the park and that old stone
church. But you slipped out of the party
too soon, just as you always threatened
you'd do. Remember being breathless
together on the observation deck of the
Empire State Building? We took the last
elevator up to the 86th floor, at 1:15 a.m.,
inhaled what drugs you had, and damn!
they were good. How dizzily I miss you
this minute in which I find myself so much
older, darling, than you ever lived to be.

Invention

Riding a ray of light, teeth bared in greeting,
I'm ready to bite, oh, anyone. In this mood,
even manure smells heady to me. A man
trapped inside me lifts weights, bulking up.
A chorus of women who hang out in my
psyche try to dissuade him from the prison
break he's got planned: *Tap into your inner
happy mammal,* they chide, *and calm down.*
"Don't mind-control me!" is his response.
Clearly, I need ancestral help. Using a spirit
phone, a device maligned as "Edison's least
successful invention," I call those I miss most
who have passed into a higher life. My mother
says the next world is packed with Jews who
worship her brisket. But if they leave the table
without being excused she scrubs their mouths
out with soap and locks them in their rooms.
My father, quiet and fair-minded in life,
confides he's applied to come back as a pirate.
Sharpening a knife, he has a strange look
on his face, and appears to have given up
shaving. *I'm hungry for the dark knowledge now,*
he growls, wiping spit from his lips with a rag
stiff with dried blood and cum. Grandma finally
learned to drive so she can run over Grandpa
with a stolen Camaro. I'm confused. This is not
what I expected from my dead, or from heaven:
relatives running amok, the celestial realm
more like some cut-rate detox program
than an ultimate reward. Enter Thomas Edison,
who hands me a dumb-looking doll. "I don't
want this stupid thing," I protest. But he won't

take it back. "I was a great man," he declares
with pride. "The Statue of Liberty's torch
went dark when I died. This doll has a tiny
phonograph record inside. Turn the crank
in her back and you'll hear human voices,
scratchy but audible. One recites the alphabet.
One sings a song about the moon. One wishes
someone good night. Don't be greedy. This is all
you get. You have much to learn about the spark
that animates inventions like this little doll,
and, most of all, about incandescence."

Animal Light

What else would I have sacrificed
to gulp more of your animal light?
Stones and clouds I shoved aside,
and sunrises and friends besides,
to watch you twist and grunt at night.
When you brushed out your feral hair,
tangled as a barroom fight,
it crackled like you were on fire.
Or was that just an arson dream,
kerosened by my desire?

Voicemail from Satan

No one is a devil if fully heard.
—Susan Sontag

So, did the claw marks on your neck heal yet?
When will I enjoy our mingled stinks again?
Better be soon. Why aren't you picking up?
Never mind. I'll find you. I just need one tuft
of your hair, a quick lick of your skin, plus
your undivided attention for several millennia.
Seriously, Flower, how are you? I gotta drop by
at least once a week till you lose your beauty.
If you're busy I'll just plop down in your den,
index afflictions, and wait. I'm gonna gnaw you
into pleasing shapes. You can deface me too.
We'll smoke some of your chatty weed. Then
you can hold my tail while I sleep, so this god-
forsaken loneliness won't overtake me.

One Who Is Always Arriving

You arrive as a limping bird who can still fly.
You arrive as an inscribed leaf I need to read.
Amid morning uproar, you arrive, riven
yet complete. You arrive at night as admonition,
as apples striving for ripeness in their bowl,
as herds lapping at a watering hole, as a torrent
of warnings and blessings, as a stream of belief
so molten that the joys, grudges, and griefs
your arrivals inspire require infinite disguises.

The Lure of the Unfinished

FOR ELISE COWEN

intercepted mid brushstroke
those who die young or trun-
cated loom   still wet with potential

those who elude us   who fled into death
their echoes gnaw at our future
and we the abandoned

remain unfinished too
friends/lovers/   interrupted
mid gesture or caress

given the slip
by loves gone to fossil or biographers' fodder
life-size paper dolls we chase through dreams

we cast them in roles they never auditioned for
blurred wrecks at rest on the seafloor
fish flit through their dissipating hulls

sentiment clouds the water
their incompleteness = infinite possibility
how ravenously I wish him back

during nights spent struggling
(without success) to decipher
his handwriting—

Having checked the *Egyptian Book of the Dead* out of the library.

I'm seized by a form of remorse. Is this the best
choice of reading for when I can't sleep, a text
crammed with fears of being eaten by animals,
of decapitation, of getting lost on the path
from demise to eternal life? I'll skip over
anxious jokes I'd planned to make here,
like, *Ha-ha, Ancients, good luck finding your esoteric
heaven with no GPS.* They painted their gods,
a jackal and falcon-headed crew, facing sideways,
as if in the midst of a line dance, tugging
reluctant mortals along by the wrist. Who isn't
horrified to rot after death, abandoned body
stinking and swelling, worms partying hard
in your corpse? In glyphs of hippopotamus
and ibis, the Ancients anticipated harms
a dead body or loosed soul was prey to,
and by naming terrors my era finds
too revolting to mention, they sought
inoculation from dangers enumerated.
They also listed perks they aimed
to maintain in the afterlife, like the pleasures
of eating and defecation. When granted
eternal life, they believed, the sun again
warms your face. The soul after death
is free to fly where it likes, bathe in the Milky
Way, take the shapes of its desires, and shimmer
as it did while it lived, shining like beaten tin
in the right light, when seen by the right eyes.

keep walking

little dust devils   kick up at your feet   whirlwinds ankle deep   take the
most delightful route home   fill your noggin with snow   or some other
clement mental weather   devise new myths and religions where
necessary   recall vanished streets and meeting places   tell the monk in
persimmon-colored robes   approaching from the opposite direction
singing with his mouth full of donated bread   what a relief it is   that his
library of guesses about the future is all wrong   yours too   o holy
mendicant what a marvel you are   skipping and stumbling   as gradually
the countryside becomes more rolling   an unearned sense of familiarity
blooms   is he an incorrect reincarnation of you   and you of him   in
that each manifests   what was banished in the other   he smells of
manhood   all day he worked harvesting pungent herbs   is it true that
love is always better than nothing   if something wondrous starts to
happen will you let it   is it too soon to tell the story of you two   working
silently together   to bury small dead animals you find by the roadside
mice and birds   where the earth is soft enough to receive them   soft as
a rough hug   you listen to him recite a few words   over hurriedly dug
tiny graves   what you feel you can't say   his verses mean no more
than fading illustrations in some book from childhood   which is
to say   everything

The Cure

Doing fantastic, thanks for asking! I just chugged
a glass of dinosaur urine and feel new baptized!
If you're ever lucky enough get your hands
on a quart of this stuff, don't be squeamish.
It makes penicillin seem like skim milk!
No virus can slay you with dino piss in your system.
Last night I participated in the eight p.m. scream-out
again. For a quarter of an hour the two halves
of my neighborhood yell as loud as they can
across our little canyon to prove to ourselves
as well as the folks we can't see anymore
that we're still kicking after nine months
of pandemic lockdown. Now my throat feels
strip-mined, but I'm glad 'cause my sense
of connection got fed—not a whole meal,
just a handful of crumbs—but hey, that's way
better than nothing. After yesterday evening's
hoot-and-holler session, a dude on the far side
of the ravine lugged a pair of ginormous speakers
up to his roof and blasted excerpts from two
of Dr. King's famous sermons, plus some lines
from a Cesar Chavez speech I could understand
only half of because, alas, my Spanish is not what I
might wish. Then he proceeded to DJ a weird-ass
menu of songs, so loud the balcony was quaking
under my feet, ranging from "Stayin' Alive" by
the squeaky-voiced Bee Gees (who *do* sound like
insects) to Aretha Franklin belting "Chain of Fools"
(a comment on the hopefully outgoing government,
was my guess). Joan Baez sang "We Shall Overcome"
in her reedy soprano. Then Aretha again with
"Amazing Grace." When I realized I could actually

see the ant-sized guy responsible for curating
this spoken-word-and-song broadcast from across
the arroyo, shirtless on his roof with a quartet
of friends, I admit I cried a little bit. Then I went
back inside and downed another mug of sauropod
pee. It's a lovely amber color, with notes of ginkgo,
horsetail, and fern. That drink sure has kept me
going during this dark time.

Downsizing

Hey, maybe the time has come to empty
your closet, get rid of your casual, business,
and formal attire, now that social occasions
have all but evaporated. Here's a nun's habit
and a negligee. That should suffice, plus a sprig
of parsley to tuck behind your ear like a gardenia
if you feel you *must* dress up during captivity.
Perhaps this sparse, nervous mustache (stickum
included) will also prove useful, for when
your boxers or panties torque into that frisky
sexual twist which means a code switch
is looming. That should do it for costumes
in your theater for one. If you want to evoke
a nostalgic mood, here's a link to staticky
radio music, and some video projections
of tree ring data for backdrop. Those were
heady years, weren't they? Meaning all
of human history. Flocks of goddesses,
their tarry mascara running. Professors
in togas which were always "accidentally"
falling open. Naked underneath, they
preached from temples or capitol steps,
claiming you'd been misled by your previous
teachers. Then they went ahead and misled
you afresh, dredging up old prejudices dressed
in new uniforms, panting out panicky rants
(while pretending to hold their togas closed),
rants of which this is but one example.

Postcard

Thanks for the shoebox full of peyote buttons.
It arrived safely, though a bit roughed up
by the post office. That spineless little cactus
has advanced my narrative! Ingesting three
buttons per day makes me feel like less of
an afterthought, shoves me deeper in love
with whoever I meet. Yesterday, for example,
Lynn showed up in her jacket with the pink
velvet collar and I was quite beside myself,
as possessed by the living spirit of her thrift-store
wrap as by her high-density self. So you see,
the peyote is obviously useful! Stories
are pouring out of me as storms through
a sieve. Tales I'd never had the heart
to tell, or in some cases even remember,
are now being beamed back to me, albeit
forcibly, via vertiginous light shows. I've
been practicing shrinking. Please return
home as soon as you graduate rehab.
That's fabulous the staff can't seem to tell
that most of you residents turn in kitten piss
for your drug tests. Sorry about the bedbugs.
Glad everyone got a new mattress. I miss
your renegade brain, your melodious,
jet-lagged laugh. Did you know the word *peyote*
derives from the Nahuatl, from a root *peyōni*,
meaning "to glisten"? You've always glistened
indispensably. You and I were chasing something.
Come back and let's see if we can catch it.

Leniency Letter

OK. I'm bowing and scraping. Apologizing
for my body and its bloat, for my wadded-up mind,
for getting drunk in my underwear so many times,
for my sense of humor which only ever bummed
everyone out. I'm sorry for changing the carnation
in my lapel twice a day. That was wasteful. I
regret not wanting what I'm supposed to want.
I'm begging pardon for singing so loudly and out
of tune on balconies when people were trying
to sleep, for never running for a bus like I meant it.
In my own defense I will say that like any spooky
moon, my head is beset with craters and dark regions.
It's easily chipped. To all the happy little plants
sprouting spiny, alien fruits who I failed to salute
each day in their noble growth as I crossed the train
tracks on my way to work, mea culpa. I feel special
remorse for populating my ark, as floodwaters
rose, turbid as a dirty martini, solely with animals
I found sexually attractive, then allowing the mouths
of some to rust shut. That was wrong. After all,
they are my kin. Are we square now? Can I go?

Wound Care Instructions

This is the inside-out of the sublime.
A bad patch, a dark phase, a rough time.
You may apply an ice pack during these days
of waiting. To the extent that you can without
lapsing into self-torture, process news from all
sources. Try not to text while jogging
so you don't end up with broken elbows
again. Do not pet dogs you haven't been
introduced to. If you don't wish to end up
with a hand so mummified in gauze it resembles
an oven mitt, slow down next time your in-laws
are due any minute for dinner and you decide
to speed-dice some onions. Take care exiting
the bath so you don't slip as you did the after-
noon of your mother's funeral and split your
forehead open on the spigot. Your attempts to
camouflage the gash with concealer yielded
a smear of makeup plus dried blood between
your eyes, which caused your aunt to ask,
"Is that mark on your head something to do
with Ash Wednesday?" Practice gratitude
because each next episode could find you
not just accident-prone but written clean out
of the series. Then your lost loves are doomed
to wander the plains of your imagination
forever. Don't suppose you're special:
everyone's shell-shocked. Give the night sky
some quality time. Never neglect the wet
blue moon. Yaks still clash at sunset. Soup,
shoes, and sure-footedness still exist. Books
and music too. So don't let yourself go. Hang
on to others tightly, nightly, till all hells

are emptied. At last, the rabbit has something
to say, so kick the cinders aside and listen.
He has that way of freezing, then trembling
mid-sentence, common to prey animals:
Finding yourself naked at the bottom of a hole
is not the worst thing. You might need to dig down
even deeper. But if you're in a dirty environment,
do keep the wound bandaged. Try not to disturb
the dressing or get it wet until morning.

Ode to the Pillow

Must a pillow, that cushiony head-welcomer, always concede to our cheeks? Can it nurse no higher ambition than to impersonate a marshmallow? Might a pillow never stand up for itself? Does it possess no intrinsic personality? Must it shun sharpness, remain nothing but slump and mush, never displaying its anger or will? The sad fact seems to be that for all its virtues, the pillow lacks backbone. Smooth and cool to the touch, clad in a fresh pillow slip, my pillow for tonight exhales a whiff of the steam iron's disciplinary rigor, but transformed, its cotton sweetening the iron's hot metal breath—the breath of a prison matron—into something more like the breath of a meadow. A shock absorber, the pillow is more forgiving than a priest (much is spilled onto it: think dream leakage). And a pillow functions well as a confessional. The sick and the helpless may be buoyed up, as if by a life raft, in clinging to their pillow, or they may be smothered with one into a final good night. Like the uncomplaining potato, the pillow is willing to take shape according to people's needs, enduring mashing after mashing. Pillows have no sense of their own splendor. Employed as ineffectual weapon, a pillow can of course burst and snow feathers, drizzle fluff or rain buckwheat husks . . . and herein lies the pillow's mysterious connection to weather. It's believed pillows subsist on a diet of mist and cloud, though no one has ever seen them eat.

Night Guidance

Some say humans become disoriented
if we go too long without seeing the light in the heavens
(light urban development drowns out . . .)

animals who navigate by the stars
are among the ones we once gave ourselves to
or became in ancient days, but we don't do that anymore
as we are struggling just to domesticate ourselves

seals complete long swims across featureless seas
guided by a constellation which describes the outline
of a giant woman, not ragingly beautiful or super sexy
but a great athlete, which angered the gods:
they're always irate about something,
if a human shows admirable talent, for example,
as if deities know terror is all they are good for

that cluster of stars over by the elm
is supposed to be an archer
imprisoned in his constellation
or some other lovesick fool

this time of year, in this hemisphere
you can clearly see Gemini:
is there hanky-panky going on
between those twins? they seem closer
than one would suppose is wholesome

when he first wakes up in the morning
his hair looks like a planetarium on fire
and that constellation yonder represents a loyal dog
delicately biting a white hibiscus,

and that one's a sunken ship
which injured its hull by hitting a whale, sadly,
not by blindsiding an iceberg
and that one's a recently defrosted mummy

streams of cosmic debris can interfere
with viewing Porcus Major, a famous constellation
representing a poorly taxidermied boar's head
a boar who is the lord of do-overs
he can grant you the ability to go back and unmake
mistakes you imagine you made
on nights when sleep was something
you could not locate
because there were no clear landmarks

Night Herons

all day long you wring yourself out
work virtually
go nowhere
brain exclusively tuned
to end-times music
till twilight arrives
to fold you in blue pleats of evening
a flock of night herons flaps past
across the sky or your mind
it's the same either way
long-closeted thoughts rise with them
winging out from daytime roosts
to forage swamps and wetlands
to nest in groups
black-crowned birds who croak like crows
swoop low over mangroves
the whir of wings
real or imagined
blurs trivial things
strange times songs declare doom looms
everyone's muzzled
mired in dread
the future's not mutual
it's mute or dead
everybody misses everybody
try to ride it out
the night herons seek
what the sun will summon us to
a prayer to be spared
after endless-seeming exile
I shall be satisfied, when I wake, with thy likeness
the night herons keep flying toward
a psalm's promise
toward all tomorrow's garlands

Acknowledgments

Thanks to these publications for publishing the following poems, sometimes in slightly different forms, sometimes with different titles:

Action, Spectacle: Sonnets 6–8 from the sequence "Fourteen Sonnets"

The Atlantic: "Marigold"

Columbia Poetry Review: "For E."

Court Green: "One Who Is Always Arriving," "Pucker and Fizz," and "The Cure"

DMQ Review: "keep walking" and "Ode to the Pillow"

Dunce Codex: "Night Guidance"

Faultline: "The Bible as Literature" and "The Story of Music"

Mississippi Review: "Schmaltz Alert"

The New Yorker: "Night Herons"

Plume: "Downsizing"

Porlock: "Leniency Letter" and "the meek"

R&R: Sonnets 1–5 from the sequence "Fourteen Sonnets"

Revel: "Postcard" and "Wound Care Instructions"

Special thanks to:

Bernard Cooper, Ruben Cota Jr., Dinah Lenney, and David Trinidad for reading this book in manuscript and making suggestions

Irina Tsoy and Tatyana Rem for keeping me alive despite my vices

Daniel Levin, Mary Storll, Lucky Benson, Bee Sacks, and Sophie Neff for being the most generous, generative writers' group on the planet and allowing me to attend same

Dennis Cooper for invaluable early education

Paul Slovak and Allie Merola for stellar editorship

Steve Gunderson for being an amazing collaborator

Francesca Gabbiani, David Lehman, Louise Steinman, Laura Berringer, and Gail Swanlund for taking an interest

Benjamin Weissman for being a true artist

Notes

Page 7 "The Bride of Frankenstein." *The Bride of Frankenstein* is the title of a 1935 film directed by James Whale.

Page 15 "Mae West Sonnet." Mae West (1893–1980) was a groundbreaking stage and film actor, singer, playwright, and screenwriter.

Page 19 "Étude." This poem was written after watching a 2020 documentary film by Lisa Rovner, *Sisters with Transistors*, which traces the history of some of the first women to make electronic music.

Page 20 "Finding Your Voice." The poem's penultimate and final lines make reference to a "golden record." NASA included golden records aboard their *Voyager* space probes, "intended to communicate a story of our world to extraterrestrials. The Voyager message is carried by a phonograph record, a 12-inch gold-plated copper disk containing sounds and images selected to portray the diversity of life and culture on Earth. . . . The contents of the record were selected for NASA by a committee chaired by Carl Sagan of Cornell University, et al. Dr. Sagan and his associates assembled 115 images and a variety of natural sounds, such as those made by surf, wind and thunder, birds, whales, and other animals. To this they added musical selections from different cultures and eras, and spoken greetings from Earth-people in fifty-five languages." See https://voyager.jpl.nasa.gov/golden-record/.

Page 22 "Some of Us Never Got Over It." The documentary film *Woodstock*, directed by Michael Wadleigh, was released in 1970. A substantially longer director's cut was released in 1994.

Page 40 "Behaving Truthfully Under Imaginary Circumstances." The poem's title quotes from legendary acting teacher Sanford Meisner, who wrote, "Acting is the ability to behave absolutely truthfully under the imaginary circumstances."

Page 56 "Invention." The poem's second line is a riff on the last line of a James Schuyler poem titled "Sleep," which reads, "Give my love to, oh, anybody."

Page 60 "One Who Is Always Arriving." The title of this poem derives from a word in the second line of a Rainer Maria Rilke poem, which is referred to by its first line, "Du im Voraus." The word is "Nimmergekommene," translated from the German by Stephen Mitchell as "You who never arrived." I have also seen it translated elsewhere as "One who never arrived."

Page 63 "keep walking" was written after watching the 1952 René Clément film *Jeux interdits* (English title: *Forbidden Games*).

Page 77 "Night Herons." The poem's last line is a tweaked version of the phrase "all tomorrow's parties," which is the title of a song by the Velvet Underground and Nico, written by Lou Reed and released as the band's debut single in 1966. The poem's fourth to last line is taken from Psalm 17:15 in the Old Testament.

About the Author

Amy Gerstler's fourteen books of poems include *Scattered at Sea* (Penguin, 2015), which was longlisted for the National Book Award, shortlisted for the Kingsley Tufts Poetry Award, and a finalist for the PEN America Literary Award; *Dearest Creature* (Penguin, 2009), which was named a *New York Times* Notable Book and shortlisted for the *Los Angeles Times* Book Prize in Poetry; and *Bitter Angel* (North Point Press, 1990), which won a National Book Critics Circle Award. She received a Guggenheim Fellowship in 2018. In 2019 she received a C.D. Wright Award from the Foundation for Contemporary Arts. She was the 2010 guest editor of the yearly anthology *The Best American Poetry*. Her work has appeared in a variety of magazines and anthologies, including *The New Yorker*, *The Paris Review*, *The American Poetry Review*, *Poetry*, several volumes of *The Best American Poetry*, and *Postmodern American Poetry: A Norton Anthology*. She has written art criticism and exhibition catalog essays for the Whitney Museum of American Art; the Museum of Contemporary Art, Los Angeles; *Artforum* magazine; and other publications.

PENGUIN POETS

GAROUS ABDOLMALEKIAN: *Lean Against This Late Hour* ✳ **PAIGE ACKERSON-KIELY:** *Dolefully, A Rampart Stands* ✳ **JOHN ASHBERY:** *Selected Poems; Self-Portrait in a Convex Mirror* ✳ **PAUL BEATTY:** *Joker, Joker, Deuce* ✳ **JOSHUA BENNETT:** *Owed; The Sobbing School; The Study of Human Life* ✳ **TED BERRIGAN:** *The Sonnets* ✳ **LAUREN BERRY:** *The Lifting Dress* ✳ **JOE BONOMO:** *Installations* ✳ **PHILIP BOOTH:** *Lifelines: Selected Poems 1950–1999; Selves* ✳ **JIM CARROLL:** *Fear of Dreaming: The Selected Poems; Living at the Movies; Void of Course* ✳ **SU CHO:** *The Symmetry of Fish* ✳ **ADRIENNE CHUNG:** *Organs of Little Importance* ✳ **RIO CORTEZ:** *Golden Ax* ✳ **MARISSA DAVIS:** *End of Empire* ✳ **ALISON HAWTHORNE DEMING:** *Genius Loci; Rope; Stairway to Heaven* ✳ **CARL DENNIS:** *Another Reason; Callings; Earthborn; New and Selected Poems 1974–2004; Night School; Practical Gods; Ranking the Wishes; Unknown Friends* ✳ **DIANE DI PRIMA:** *Loba* ✳ **STUART DISCHELL:** *Backwards Days; Dig Safe* ✳ **STEPHEN DOBYNS:** *Velocities: New and Selected Poems 1966–1992* ✳ **EDWARD DORN:** *Way More West* ✳ **HEID E. ERDRICH:** *Little Big Bully* ✳ **ROGER FANNING:** *The Middle Ages* ✳ **ADAM FOULDS:** *The Broken Word: An Epic Poem of the British Empire in Kenya, and the Mau Mau Uprising Against It* ✳ **CARRIE FOUNTAIN:** *Burn Lake; Instant Winner; The Life* ✳ **AMY GERSTLER:** *Dearest Creature; Ghost Girl; Index of Women; Is This My Final Form?; Medicine; Nerve Storm; Scattered at Sea* ✳ **EUGENE GLORIA:** *Drivers at the Short-Time Motel; Hoodlum Birds; My Favorite Warlord; Sightseer in This Killing City* ✳ **DEBORA GREGER:** *In Darwin's Room* ✳ **ZEINA HASHEM BECK:** *O* ✳ **TERRANCE HAYES:** *American Sonnets for My Past and Future Assassin; Hip Logic; How to Be Drawn; Lighthead; So to Speak; Wind in a Box* ✳ **NATHAN HOKS:** *The Narrow Circle* ✳ **ROBERT HUNTER:** *Sentinel and Other Poems* ✳ **MARY KARR:** *Viper Rum* ✳ **W. B. KECKLER:** *Sanskrit of the Body* ✳ **JACK KEROUAC:** *Book of Blues; Book of Haikus; Book of Sketches* ✳ **JOANNA KLINK:** *Circadian; Excerpts from a Secret Prophecy; The Nightfields; Raptus* ✳ **JOANNE KYGER:** *As Ever: Selected Poems* ✳ **ANN LAUTERBACH:** *Door; Hum; If in Time: Selected Poems 1975–2000; On a Stair; Or to Begin Again; Spell; Under the Sign* ✳ **CORINNE LEE:** *Plenty; Pyx* ✳ **PHILLIS LEVIN:** *May Day; Mr. Memory & Other Poems* ✳ **PATRICIA LOCKWOOD:** *Motherland Fatherland Homelandsexuals* ✳ **WILLIAM LOGAN:** *Rift of Light* ✳ **J. MICHAEL MARTINEZ:** *Museum of the Americas; Tarta Americana* ✳ **ADRIAN MATEJKA:** *The Big Smoke; Map to the Stars; Mixology; Somebody Else Sold the World* ✳ **AMBER McBRIDE:** *Thick with Trouble* ✳ **MICHAEL McCLURE:** *Huge Dreams: San Francisco and Beat Poems* ✳ **ROSE McLARNEY:** *Colorfast; Forage; Its Day Being Gone* ✳ **DAVID MELTZER:** *David's Copy: The Selected Poems of David Meltzer* ✳ **TERESA K. MILLER:** *Borderline Fortune* ✳ **ROBERT MORGAN:** *Dark Energy; Terroir* ✳ **CAROL MUSKE-DUKES:** *Blue Rose; An Octave Above Thunder: New and Selected Poems; Red Trousseau; Twin Cities* ✳ **ALICE NOTLEY:** *Being Reflected Upon; Certain Magical Acts; Culture of One; The Descent of Alette; Disobedience; For the Ride; In the Pines; Mysteries of Small Houses* ✳ **WILLIE PERDOMO:** *The Crazy Bunch; The Essential Hits of Shorty Bon Bon* ✳ **DANIEL POPPICK:** *Fear of Description* ✳ **LIA PURPURA:** *It Shouldn't Have Been Beautiful* ✳ **LAWRENCE RAAB:** *The History of Forgetting; Visible Signs: New and Selected Poems* ✳ **BARBARA RAS:** *The Last Skin; One Hidden Stuff* ✳ **M.S. REDCHERRIES:** *mother* ✳ **MICHAEL ROBBINS:** *Alien vs. Predator; The Second Sex; Walkman* ✳ **PATTIANN ROGERS:** *Flickering; Generations; Holy Heathen Rhapsody; Quickening Fields; Wayfare* ✳ **SAM SAX:** *Madness* ✳ **ROBYN SCHIFF:** *Information Desk: An Epic; A Woman of Property* ✳ **WILLIAM STOBB:** *Absentia; Nervous Systems* ✳ **TRYFON TOLIDES:** *An Almost Pure Empty Walking* ✳ **VINCENT TORO:** *Hivestruck; Tertulia* ✳ **PAUL TRAN:** *All the Flowers Kneeling* ✳ **SARAH VAP:** *Viability* ✳ **ANNE WALDMAN:** *Gossamurmur; Kill or Cure; Manatee/Humanity; Mesopotopia; Trickster Feminism* ✳ **JAMES WELCH:** *Riding the Earthboy 40* ✳ **PHILIP WHALEN:** *Overtime: Selected Poems* ✳ **PHILLIP B. WILLIAMS:** *Mutiny* ✳ **MIA S. WILLIS:** *the space between men* ✳ **ROBERT WRIGLEY:** *Anatomy of Melancholy and Other Poems; Beautiful Country; Box; Earthly Meditations: New and Selected Poems; Lives of the Animals; Reign of Snakes; The True Account of Myself as a Bird* ✳ **MARK YAKICH:** *The Importance of Peeling Potatoes in Ukraine; Spiritual Exercises; Unrelated Individuals Forming a Group Waiting to Cross*